A to Z PPC

Written by

Jordon Meyer

Illustrated by

Nataliia Tymoshenko
Maggie Liesch

BookPress®

A to Z PPC makes it fun
to learn your **ABC**s.

Search and Click on that Googy Ad.

Written and launched by Mom or Dad.

CPC or CPV, let's turn these
pages with frequency.

G is for
Google

K is for

tiger shark

tiger king

eye of the tiger lyrics

Key word

tiger lily

detroit tigers

tony the tiger

tasmanian tiger

crouching tiger hidden dragon

daniel tiger

O is for
Opportunities
Tab

Q is for Quality Score

R is for

Remarketing

ogle   bedazzled boots

S

is
for

Search
Engine
Results
Page

U is for User Access

W is for **Website**

X is for
X-Out Those
Notifications

How many magnifying glasses can you find hidden in the pages of this book?

How many magnifying glasses
are in this book?

The answer is 23.

How many did you find?

Great job with your ABCs!

About the Author

Jordon Meyer is a PPC expert practitioner and the Founder and CEO of Granular, a leading digital marketing agency based in Milwaukee, Wisconsin. Prior to starting Granular, Jordon spent the previous ten years in various leadership roles, serving as the "go-to" digital marketing expert responsible for driving measurable revenue growth for various companies in the Midwest including Best Buy, Globe University, Lightburn, and Zeon Solutions. He has personally managed a digital marketing budget of over $40 million, worked on more than a hundred brands, and led three in-house marketing teams. Jordon lives in Milwaukee's Bay View neighborhood with his wife Jaime and two mini dachshunds named Oscar Meyer and Bluth.

Published by: Bookpress Publishing • P.O. Box 71532, Des Moines, IA 50325 • www.BookpressPublishing.com

Publisher's Cataloging-in-Publication Data

Names: Meyer, Jordon M., author. | Tymoshenko, Natalia, illustrator. | Liesch, Maggie, illustrator.
Title: A to Z PPC / by Jordon M. Meyer; illustrated by Nataliia Tymoshenko and Maggie Liesch.
Description: Des Moines, IA: Bookpress Publishing, 2023. | Summary: A fun way for kids to learn their ABCs using words from the digital advertising world.
Identifiers: LCCN: 2022915851 | ISBN: 978-1-947305-55-7
Subjects: LCSH Advertising--Juvenile literature. | Advertising and children--Juvenile literature. | Young consumers--Juvenile literature. | Alphabet. | BISAC JUVENILE NONFICTION / Business & Economics
Classification: LCC HF5829 .M49 2023 | DDC 659.1--dc23

First Edition
Printed in the United States of America
10 9 8 7 6 5 4 3 2 1